BADGER'S GOLF COMPENDIUM

Badger's Golf Compendium

The Essential Illustrated Handbook for Clubhouse Bores

Niall Edworthy

Illustrations by Mudd Bexley

Publisher: Badger Books

Copyright: © Niall Edworthy

Niall Edworthy has asserted his right under the Copyright, Designs
and Patents Act 1988 to be identified as the author of this work

All illustrations copyright: © Mudd Bexley

ISBN: 978-1-7384522-4-8

eBook ISBN: 978-1-7384522-5-5

Book design by Principal Publishing

nialledworthy.com

Addressing the Ball – i) Tense moment before the swing when the golfer is sure the body, clubface and feet are all in perfect synch before executing the **Waggle** ii) Undiplomatic language bellowed after the ball as it slices horribly, cannons off a tree and slaps into the water

Hacker – *Derog.* A crude player, either new to the game or plain useless, sometimes uncouth, just in it for the chat and the beers in the clubhouse. See also **Duffer, Chopper**

CONTENTS

Foreword

There are close to 450 golfing words and phrases contained within these pages. The extreme golf 'Badger' (See also Golf Buff, User, Bore, Fiend) will probably be familiar with a great many. I hope they may still be surprised by a good number of the entries, partly because they have been drawn from all corners of the global golfing 'community' and partly because new words and expressions are constantly emerging.

Either way, I hope that it is the definition given to these terms that will grant the book its appeal. If nothing else, golf is a game rich in humour and gentle mockery, and I have tried to celebrate that. So, we have here the timeless, universal humour that bonds all golfers – plus the satisfaction of having all that terminology collected into one handy volume for the loo, coffee table or golf bag. Some may find the handbook useful for a quick reference and refresher before heading out for a round and slinging some invective at their playing partner. It's a dipper, not an A-to-Z read.

The problem with jokes is that they are often forgotten as soon as they are heard, so I hope too that this collection acts as some form of permanent record, a kind of Humour Hansard for the expressions, exchanges and exclamations that are uttered at clubs and across fairways every day.

I have also included many of the more technical terms commonly used, if not always understood, and translated them into the language of the lay golfer. If you had never played or followed golf, I would like to think that by the time you read every entry, you would have a pretty good idea of the game's culture and how it plays out on the course.

Few sports lend themselves to comedy like golf. Planning this series of humorous sports glossaries, the golfers amongst my friends immediately put up their hands and went into comedy routines, reeling off term after humorous term. Some of these people I had never previously suspected of being amusing. It took golf to bring out their inner stand-up.

Golf produces so much rich and amusing phraseology for two main reasons. First, it is a fiddly, difficult, technical game. With all that failure, fear and frustration, it is inevitable that dark, cynical, self-deprecating humour will abound. Second, though a team sport only rarely, golf is collegiate, convivial, clubbable.

Every tribe develops a distinctive language of its own. Homo Golfer, an ancient, diverse and widespread group settled on every continent bar Antarctica, is no different. Many of the game's terms and idioms can be traced back centuries, and new ones are turning up all the time, not least from the world of technology, spread rapidly by a proliferating media.

Where you find a man in colourful slacks and caps hacking and huffing in the sand and shrubbery, you will find banter. And where there is a clubhouse with a generous bar, you have the ideal venue for ridicule and repartee. Truth is, I could have added another half a dozen or so pages to this book. Had the constraints of the righteous society that lies beyond the course and clubhouse been lifted – or I had been bold enough – I could have added scores of the more ribald, hilarious and distinctly un-PC words and expressions from golf's lexicon of the vernacular.

For fear of being put in the stocks on the village green, I have been obliged to omit the worst offenders. The defence that I am only reporting what golfers utter every day would, I fear, be insufficient mitigation. Someone wearing badges would track me down, stick a cream pie in my face and tell me I am going to die in the flames of Hell.

But don't despair. In the absence of our more offensive friends, take comfort in knowing that the language of golf remains perfectly funny and curious without them.

NE, Chichester 2024

Abbreviations

Arch. – Archaic

Brit. – British

Cru. – Cruel

Derog. – Derogatory

Sco. – Scottish

U.S. – American

Vulg. – Vulgar

A

Aboard - On the green, no longer floundering in an ocean of rough

Abominable Snowman – Nine shots or worse on a hole. See also **Snowman**

Acceleration – i) Increase of clubhead speed in the downswing ii) Speeding up over the last few holes to hit the clubhouse bar

Ace – A hole-in-one, straight in the cup from the tee. A triumph the player will wear like imperial laurels, boring playing players, spouse, work colleagues and strangers on the street until his deathbed. He might even buy a round of drinks for his playing partners

Across the Line – Staple swing error of the casual golfer resulting in a slice or pull, caused by poor positioning of the club at the top of the backswing, triggering instant self-loathing

Alignment – More abstract theory than concrete reality for most golfers, this describes the harmonious positioning of body and club to hit the correct target line

Addressing the Ball – i) Tense moment before the swing when the golfer is sure the body, clubface and feet are all in perfect synch before executing the **Waggle**

ii) Undiplomatic language bellowed after the ball as it slices horribly, cannons off a tree and slaps into the water

Adolf Hitler – Two shots in the bunker

Afraid of the Dark – Of a putt that won't drop

Aircraft Carrier – The teeing area or box when it is raised like a stage or a mini-plateau from where the more accomplished golfer will launch his drive with military accuracy straight down the fairway for the perfect lie and approach shot

Airmail – Of a ball that flies over green or any shot that travels further than intended

Air Shot – Golfer's nightmare. A Chaplinesque swing and a miss. Cue awkward shuffling of feet, crimsoning of cheeks and clearing of throats. The shame will destroy the **Duffer's** inner peace for the rest of the round and probably the rest of the week

Albatross – Three shots under par for a hole. An extremely rare accomplishment most golfers will never witness, let alone achieve. See also **Double Eagle**

Alec Guinness – *Brit*. A shot that goes out of bounds or 'OB', as it is recorded. As in Obi Wan Kenobi, the character played by Guinness in *Star Wars*

Amelia Earhart – *Cru*. A shot that looks good in the air then disappears. After the American aviation pioneer whose Lockheed Electra disappeared over the Pacific in 1927 during her bid to circumnavigate the globe

Amen Corner – Difficult hole, or the stretch of one. Pray and hit

Apron – The fringe or 'collar' of the green where the grass is shorter than the fairway but longer than the putting green. See also **Frog Hair, Peach Fuzz**

Army Golf – Inaccurate shot play, marching over the course and hitting the ball *left-right, left-right, left-right*

Armpit – The tangle of rough in the angle of a dogleg

Ash, Leslie – *Brit. Cru.* A big lip-out when a putt rotates wildly around the cup and shoots away. An unkind reference to the traumatic lip-filler procedure suffered by the popular British actress

B

Back Country – A land far beyond the fairway

Backhander – i) Tapping in the ball next to the hole with the back of a putter ii) A sly compliment that undermines while appearing to flatter

Backpacker – The player heading off to the Back Country to find his ball

Back Nine – The last nine holes often walked in a dispirited trudge

Backspin – Applying reverse rotation of the ball to give it lift, stability in the flight and grip on ground impact to reduce the roll. Sounds easy, hard to execute. Usually accidental with the casual golfer

Back Tilt – Slight angling of the upper body for putting and short game shots (Good). Leaning back too far and goofing the shot (Bad)

Back Weighting the Irons – Design comfort for the rookie and the hapless. Adding weight to the rear of the club head to win a little forgiveness from the club, achieve greater height in the shot and provide a more solid feel

Backwoodsman – A player who spends much of his round hacking his ball out from the trees. See Also **Tree Hugger**

Bad Lie – i) Ball sitting in a dismal position ii) Telling people you play off scratch

Baffing Spoon or Baffie – *Sco. Arch.* Obsolete fairway wood used for loft and to escape difficult lies

Bailout – Safety shot, either to avoid a hazard or to set up for the harder one next up

Banana Ball – A drive curving sharply away from its intended line, its flightpath shaped like the world's most popular fruit

7

Bandit – *Derog*. Villainous player who lies about his skill level to win money or prestige. See Also **Hustler, Sandbagger**

Barkie – When a golfer salvages par after striking a tree

Beach, On the – In the bunker

Belly Putter – A long-shafted putter the player grips around the abdomen in order to make himself look stupid. Like walking poles for the hiker, the belly putter can be a sensible and practical option, but it's not a great look, suggesting a lack of confidence and basic skills. See also **Broomstick, Chest Putter**

Bentgrass – Common-or-garden golf grass. Of the *Agrostis* genus, it is found on putting greens, tees and the better fairways. It is favoured for its thin blades, dense growth, pleasingly dark appearance, and ability to withstand foot traffic. It will also take a close mow without complaint, offering a smooth, speedy finish to the surface. What's not to like about Bentgrass?

Best Ball – A game format, A.k.a. Better Ball or Four-ball, by which the lowest score on each hole is logged. See also **Scramble**

Biarritz Green – A massive green with a deep 'swale' or gully running across it, typically flanked by long, narrow bunkers. Named for the green of the 3rd hole at the fashionable Phare Club in the southwest France resort town, once popular with wealthy Britons, including King Edward VII. Dubbed 'the Chasm', the green no longer exists. It has a hotel on it.

Big Rig – The large cart bag on a golf cart stuffed with unnecessary equipment that never gets used

Bingo, Bango, Bongo – i) Points-based game. Bingo for the first player on the green, Bango for the first closest to the pin and Bongo for first in the hole ii) Terrible Frank Sinatra song about 'savages' in the Congo jungle

Birdie – One stroke under par for a hole. Origin unknown, but possibly from the old US slang word 'bird' denoting something good

Birdie Dance – Player's celebration after holing his putt for a one-under-par

Bite – Describing the backspin on a ball

Blade – A.k.a. **Muscleback**. Thin iron with a flat face and a small sweet spot. No, that's not an un-PC joke. This is the club for the accomplished golfer or the braver one, seeking more control and less forgiveness for their effort. The opposite of the weighted iron

Blast – Shot played from a greenside bunker when the ball is buried in sand and demands some welly behind it. The subsequent eruption of sand creates the impression of a blast. **See also Explosion Shot**

Blind Shot – Played when the golfer's view has been blocked or obscured by an obstruction caused by the topography of the course - a hill, woodland, or dogleg - or by the gallon of claret drunk at lunch

Blocking Shot – When a (right-handed) ~~muppet~~ golfer aims to the right of the target, the ball travels in a straight line and keeps going, the intended curve never comes, and the ball lands somewhere dreadful. It is caused by any number of faults in the set-up, but usually, because the club face has been too open. A.k.a. **Push Shot**

Bloodsomes – Foursome format, a variation of Scramble, in which one pair selects the worst of their opponents' tee shots for them to play next— i.e. a perfect game for low handicappers who've enjoyed a good drink. High handicappers will be kicked off the course for slow play. The cruel fun of the game lies in making opponents play a ball buried in a bunker or lost in the gorse. A.k.a. Gruesomes

Bogey Golfer – A player who is typically one over par on most holes. Solid, average

Bolan, Marc – *Cru. Brit.* Heartless expression for a shot that hits a tree. Named for the British glam rock lead singer of T-Rex, who died when his girlfriend's Mini crashed into a tree on Barnes Common, London, in 1977

Bomb & Gouge – New-ish expression emerging from the modern emphasis on power hitting and distance, the player going for length of drive, and to hell with the consequences -- Rambo will just smash it out of the rough

Borrow – To adjust the line of a putt, taking into account the slope and contours of a green

Botox – When a putt takes a fat lip around the hole

Brassie – *Arch. Sco.* Obsolete term for a 2-wood used to play the ball off a fairway. The club took its name from the brass underplate of the club. Originally called a 'rut iron' or 'track iron' because, in the early days, golf was played on common land traversed by farm carts, often carrying loads of seaweed and sand that left deep ruts in the sodden Scottish earth

Brazilian – *Vulg.* Common mischievous word for a putt that shaves the hole, provoking sniggers on the green

Break – How the ball changes direction over the contour or kink of a green

Breakfast Ball – A type of **Mulligan** when a player in a social game is granted a second drive off the first tee after a shocking first effort as a result of it being so early in the morning he hasn't woken up to the fact he is playing golf

Broccoli Beater – The player spending much of his round in the rough

Broomstick – Longer and even sillier-looking than a **Belly Putter**, the club is held with one hand at the top and the other anchoring it lower down, like someone sweeping a floor. No golfer looks cool with a broomstick putter. See also **Chest Putter**

Bump and Run – Approach shot to the green where the player dinks a low chip and scoots the ball along the ground towards the green

Buried – The unhappy state of affairs when the ball finds itself deep in tall grass or sand

Buried Elephant – Massive hump on the putting green

Businessman's Grip – *Derog.* As displayed by the inexperienced or part-time player

Buzzard – A double bogey or two-over par on a hole, the buzzard is a term that is not uttered as often as it is experienced. Sometimes misheard as the exclamation, 'Bastard!'

C

Cabbage – Deep rough. See also **Goat's Breakfast, Jungle, Spinach**

Caddie Master – Grumpy old-timer in charge of detailing caddies to players

Calcutta – Auction-style betting system in which the players in a social or charity tournament bid on those they think are going to play the best

Camel – *Derog.* Long-faced, bad-tempered player who spends half his round on the sand of the bunker

Campbell, Alastair – *Brit.* Too much spin. Named for former UK Prime Minister Tony Blair's master of the dark arts of news manipulation and PR 'spin'

Can, In the – Ball in the hole

Cape Hole – A green jutting out into a lake, pond or sea, presenting a nerve-jangling approach for players.

With water on three sides, the player has a stark choice of playing it safe or going for broke and ending up with a **Red October**

Captain Kirk – A wild shot, going where no shot has gone before

Carpet, On the – Ball safely on the fairway or green where the grass is lovely, short and smooth

Carry – i) Distance a shot travels ii) To transport the bag on the shoulder rather than pull it on a trolley iii) What a player does for his hopeless partner in a game of Foursomes

Carry Bag – Light golf bag with a few clubs for a quick, informal round. See also **Sunday Bag**

Cart Girl – Everyone's favourite course employee. The Good Samaritan who drives around in a cart selling beer, nuts and chocolate

Cart Jockey – The guy forever pootling around the course in a moon buggy. Employee or greenkeeper on a golf course

Casual Water – Big rain puddles splashed across the fairway, waiting to swallow your ball

Casting - One of multiple types of swing error, in this instance, when the player loses the stiff hinge of his wrist too early and throws the clubface at the ball. The same mistake is made by rod fishermen when releasing the line into the water

Cat Box – Sand bunker. See also **Kitty Litter**

Cavity Back – A bulkier iron with an area scooped out of the back of the club head for a larger **Sweet Spot,** favoured by lesser players for its ease of use and greater forgiveness than the thin **Blades** preferred by more experienced players

Chef – Player who keeps slicing the ball

Chef's Salad – An area of rough containing a diversity of flora

Chest Putter – Similar to the **Broomstick** with its extended shaft, but anchored against the chest rather than the chin

Chicken Stick – Any club apart from a driver for teeing off, the taunt

16

being that the player has chickened out of going for the riskier option

Chicken Wing – Swing malfunction when the leading elbow flexes away from the body

Chilli Dip – Striking the ground before the ball, digging out some dirt in the manner of a corn chip plunging into a bowl of guacamole. See also **Fat Shot**

Chip & Run – Shot, usually to clear an obstacle and achieve a bit of distance along the fairway

Chippers – Hybrid golf club, part putter, part iron, for dinking the ball onto the green

Choke Down – i) Grip the club further down to hit the ball a shorter distance ii) To swallow your self-loathing after an appalling round

Chopper – A wretched player. See also **Hacker, Duffer**

Christmas Present – Ball under a tree

Church Pews – A bunker with rows of raised strips of turf

Claggy Lie – *Brit*. A ball lying miserably in sticky mud

Claw Putting – Putting technique for greater stability where the lower hand is not wrapped around the grip but looser, the fingers pointing down at an angle and acting as a stabiliser. Once mocked as an act of desperation by a confidence-shot player with the **Yips**, several leading players have since deployed the grip

Cleek – *Arch. Sco.* An old form of fairway iron, equivalent to a No.1 or No. 2 for long low shots. The term probably comes from the Scots word for the heavy iron hook used to hang pots over fires

Comebacker – The putt required when the previous one has passed the hole

Condor – Fantasy word to describe a hole-in-one on a Par 5

Condom – *Vulg.* A shot felt to be safe but unsatisfying

Corbyn, Jeremy – *Brit.* Too far left. Refers to the former Labour Party leader, who suffered a landslide defeat in the UK's 2019 General Election. Considered too far left even for his left-wing party, if he was a golf ball, he went out of bounds

Cross-handed – Putting grip with the left hand under the right (for the right-hander). Similar to the position when being handcuffed by the police.

Cuban – A ball just short of the hole that needed another revolution to get in. See **Corbyn, Jeremy**

D

Dance Floor, On the – Ball on the putting green

Dawn Patrol – Early tee-off. See **Dew Sweepers**

Decel – i) When the club slows – decelerates - in the downswing, leading to a failure to follow through, an unwelcome development not to be encouraged. See **Quitting the Swing** ii) The slowing down of a round occasioned by the uselessness, indolence or fading interest of the participants

Deepage – Distant lands reached by the longer drive

Depth Charge – A long putt down a challenging slope played with the limited aim of getting into the vicinity of the hole rather than in expectation of scoring a direct hit of the target. See also **Lag Putt**

Derek, Bo – Ten shots or more on a hole, referencing Bo's appearance in the 1979 romantic comedy *10* in which Dudley Moore's character, who rates women with marks out of ten, becomes infatuated with Bo's character, Jenny

DeVito, Danny – Five-footer putt

Dew Sweepers – Early morning players. See **Dawn Patrol**

Diego – *Brit*. A very nasty little five-footer. Of a putt. Refers to Argentinian footballer Diego 'Hand of God' Maradona, nemesis of English football

Dimples – Pockmarks on a golf ball

Dog Leg – A hole that bends sharply in the manner of a dog's hind leg

Dog Track – *Derog*. Scruffy, low-quality course. See also **Goat Track**

Dormie – Scoring term in match play format indicating that a player or team leads by the same number of remaining holes. Supposedly, but not certainly, from the French 'Dormir', suggesting the leaders can sleep their way through the last holes

Down the Middle, Cyril – Hit the tee shot down the centre of the fairway

Downswing – Where it all goes wrong for so many. When the clubhead descends from the top of the swing, accelerating towards its fateful impact with the ball

Double Eagle – A collector's item rare as a dog's egg when someone scores a two on a Par 5. See also **Albatross**

Double Tap – i) When a player mistakenly hits the ball twice, incurring a penalty ii) Two firearm shots in rapid succession to neutralise an enemy or suspect at close quarters, rare on golf courses

Douglas Bader – *Cru*. Looks brilliant in the air but doesn't have the legs. Cruel reference to the British

Spitfire ace who had both legs amputated after a flying accident before the war

DQ – Scoreboard abbreviation for Disqualified. Sometimes used as a verb, such as 'He was DQ'd for failing to sign his scorecard.'

Drain a Putt – Get it in the hole

Draw – A deliberate shot-shape where the right-handed golfer applies some side spin to bring the ball's trajectory back to the centre. You ask, 'Why not just hit it straight, fool?' Because, obvs, the draw will generate more distance in carry and roll from the curve of the ball

Dribbler – i) A mishit when the ball rolls a bit ii) The weird-looking guy in the shrubbery of a municipal course

Duck Hook – A poorly executed shot that bends wildly. A.k.a. Snap Hook

Duff – A poor shot. See **Duffer**

Duffer – *Derog.* Player who hits a lot of Duffs. See also **Chopper, Hacker**

E

Eagle – Two under par on a hole, the superlative of a little **Birdie**

Etiquette – Rules of propriety and decorum. Observed by some players

Eva Braun – Picked up in a bunker

Executive Course – Shorter course with more Par 3s suitable for lunch breaks and important meetings

Explosion Shot – Spraying the sand when hitting a buried ball from the bunker. See **Blast**

F

Fade – i) Common shot where the ball starts left and comes back towards the centre, deployed to negotiate obstacles and hold the ball against the wind ii) Of a player's performance after a bright start

Fat Shot – Hitting the ground before the ball and spooning the dirt. See also **Chilli Dip**

Ferret – *Brit.* A ball that goes straight into the hole from outside the green without touching the ground, disappearing from view like the domesticated polecat down a rat hole

Fescue – Tall, tough ornamental grass found along fairways, mainly on unmown areas of coastal courses, favoured by greenkeepers for its ability to thrive on sandy and poor soils and its resistance to drought. It doesn't mind a skinhead mow either, so can also be used on fairways and even greens

First Cut – i) The light rough on the outer edges of the fairway ii) The trimming or halving of the tournament, usually after the first two rounds

Fish – The player always finding the water

Flange – Lovely, wasted word signifying the part of an iron sticking out from the back of the clubhead. It would be better off describing a pudding. What golfer ever says, 'Hey, check out the flange on this beauty?'

Flatstick – Slang for putter

Flier Shot – When a ball is impeded in the light rough, and the only option is to give it a good thump high into the air. With minimal spin control possible and the strong risk of overshooting the target, the flier shot doesn't always end happily on the **Dance Floor**

Flop – i) A high-arcing shot, played with an open stance and club-face, to get over an obstacle or when there is only a miserly area of green to hit. A.k.a. Lob ii) Loser, deadbeat, dud, also-ran, turkey, boob

Flub – Semi-poetic word describing a badly mishit shot, stirring images of an imbecile with his tongue hanging out, drooling down his club shaft

Fluffy Lie – In the light rough

Flush Hit – In the sweet spot, straight out of the screws

Flusher – A putt that circles the hole before dropping in the manner of a siphonic lavatory bowl

Fly the Green – Extreme overhit when the ball *lands* on the far side of the green, the result of a malfunction in the player's distance calculator. See Also **Airmail**

Follow Through – The final phase of the swing after contact. The ball is already in transit, so a good follow-through can do little to influence its fate. So, it is more that the final flourish confirms that everything before it has been executed well. A jerky or wild follow-through will indicate that the player's entire swing action needs serious examination

Foot Flare – When a player's feet point out at an angle rather than straight ahead, as they should when addressing the ball. Away from a golf course, this is what is meant by being flat-footed or having 'duck feet.'

Foot Wedge – The invisible club carried by all corrupt golfers, perfect for a sneaky, illegal kick of the ball for a better lie

Fore! – Bellowed alert to warn the players further up the fairway of a dangerous incoming ball. Believed to have been adopted from the cry of artillery gunners to the infantry to drop to the ground before firing

Forgiveness – i) The user-friendly design of a club that helps mitigate an imperfectly struck shot that has failed to find the sweet spot ii) Pardoning your partner for playing like a **Duffer** or your opponent for deploying his **Foot Wedge**

Four Jack – Four putts on a hole

Free Drop – Granted, without penalty, to a player whose ball has landed in an area that is unfairly unplayable, e.g. a cart path or on ground under repair

Frenchie – i) The happy moment when the gods offer mercy and a wildly struck ball cannons off a tree trunk back onto the fairway. Origin unknown. ii) The kiss you won't get from the spouse after a day on the golf course

Fried-Egg Lie – When a ball has plopped from on high into the bunker, radiating a circle of sand to create the vague impression of an egg in a frying pan. See also **Plugged Lie**

Fringe – The area around the green that is neither green nor fairway. See also **Apron, Frog Hair, Peach Fuzz**

Front Nine – Where it all begins so promisingly: the rolling fairways, the woodlands, a warm sun and light breeze, the company of friends, new slacks, away from the office or the chores at home … what could go wrong?

G

Garden Course – *U.S.* A beautiful, well-manicured course, a feast for the eyes landscaped with flowering shrubbery, specimen trees and distinctive plants. Augusta, Georgia, host of the Masters, is the best-known garden course with its famous 'Azalea' 13th hole and abundant Magnolias, Camellias and Dogwoods

Gardening – Fixing a divot

Gator Country – The rough in Florida

Gerry Adams – *Brit.* Banter term for a provisional ball, Adams being an Irish Republican politician, former President of Sinn Fein and commander in the Provisional Irish Republican Army, or Provos. See **Provisional, Happy Ball**

Gilligan – Fun rule when you can make your opponent play his shot again

Gimme – Either an easy tap-in to the hole or when the ball is so close to it, the opponent concedes the stroke and gives the putt. A customary act of sportsmanship in casual games, the failure to grant a Gimme will lead to a cooling in diplomatic relations over the rest of the round

Glenn Miller – *Cru*. A ball that keeps low and ends in the water. Wicked reference to the death of the American bandleader and troop entertainer whose aircraft disappeared crossing the English Channel in 1944

Goat's Breakfast – The rough. See also **Cabbage, Jungle, Spinach**

Goat Track – *Derog*. A golf course in deplorable condition, as though chewed and trampled by a herd of ruminant billies, nannies and kids. See also **Dog Track**

Goldie – The favourable bounce that rescues a shot from a dire fate. See also **Frenchie**

Golf Twat – *Derog*. Like a normal twat but plays golf a lot

Gooseneck – A.k.a. Plumber's Neck. A type of putter or iron with a kink in the hosel above the clubface

Gorse – Where you do not want your shot to land. Widespread in the UK and abundant on Scottish courses, the spikes of the bright yellow-flowering evergreen shrub will shred the skin of any golfer foolish enough to try and play out from a thicket of it. Take a drop instead, and enjoy the rest of the round without medical treatment

Grain – The alignment of grass blades on a green that influences a putt's speed and movement. Greenkeepers talk of the grain of Velvet Bentgrass as a bespoke cabinetmaker will talk of cherry wood

Grasscutter – A powerful, fizzing shot that never gets off the ground

Green Jacket – The ultimate prize in Men's golf, coveted more for the achievement it represents than its fashion virtues, this smart casual lounge coat is the traditional award for the winner of the US Masters at Augusta. Often ill-fitting, but the winner will have his own tailored after the event

Greenies – i) Short for 'greens in regulation', this is the stat that measures whether a player reaches the green in the expected number of strokes, e.g. a par 3 in one shot, a par 4 in two. ii) Side bet as to who hits the ball closest to the green or pin

Grooves – Cool word for the light furrows on an iron clubface to assist spin. Golfers rarely discuss their grooves

Grind – i) Altering the sole of a club, usually a wedge, to suit the player's game ii) A tough round in the company of someone disagreeable

Grinder – The man who grinds. Not to be confused with the dating website

Grips – Three main types: The Vardon Overlap is the most popular amongst Pros, the Interlocking for players with small hands, and the Baseball for beginners with all ten fingers on the club

Gross –Score before handicap is taken into account

Gynaecologist's Assistant – *Vulg*. Risqué expression for a putt that shaves the hole. Rarely heard on Presbyterian courses

H

Hacker – *Derog.* A crude player, either new to the game or plain useless, sometimes uncouth, just in it for the chat and the beers in the clubhouse. See also **Duffer, Chopper**

Hail Mary Shot – A hit-and-hope effort against all the odds, usually when the player is in a desperate situation and in need of a miracle. See also **Amen Corner**

Halfway House – The favourite feature of a course for the reluctant golfer – the shack or tea hut after the 9th hole serving snacks and hot beverages

Hammer Hands – The clumsy oaf who putts like he has mallets for hands

Hand Wedge – Picking up the ball and putting it somewhere with a more favourable lie. Cheating, of course, but who's looking?

Handicap – i) The system by which a player's skill level is measured to allow golfers of varying competence to play against each other without getting too bored or too embarrassed ii) Any one of multiple issues likely affecting a player's ability to play well

Handsy – Too much wrist in the swing

Hangman – The terrible score of nine on a hole, so-called owing to the numeral's resemblance to a man hanging from a noose

Hangtime – The period that the ball spends in the air

Happy Ball – A provisional ball played when the original is feared lost. See also **Gerry Adams**

Happy Gilmore – A clownish shot made for laughs during a casual round or exhibition charity game. The shot is played by running at the ball and scything a wild swing at it. Named for the Adam Sandler character in the eponymous film in which a hapless, angry ice hockey player becomes a Pro golfer

Hardpan Lie – A ball sitting on baked earth waiting to give your wrists a painful jolt

Heel it – Striking the ball with the area of the clubface close to the shaft. Rarely produces a happy outcome

Hogan, Ben to Hogan, Hulk – Playing like a golfing god one minute, then inexplicably turning into a clumsy wrestler. Ben Hogan, one of the all-time greats; Hulk Hogan, a floor-grappler in red tights and yellow singlet with a comedy moustache, born by no small irony in Augusta, Georgia

Hitting the Big Ball before the Little Ball – Taking a chunk out of the Earth

Hit a Brick – A putt that stops abruptly before the hole

Hold the Green – When the ball hits the green and stays there

Honour – The privilege of teeing off

Hook – A shot that heads in one direction and, owing to the spin imparted, usually unintentional, curves back towards the player. The hook is an extreme form of the 'draw' moving right to left for the right-handed player

Hosel – What you hit when you shank a shot: the part of the club that attaches the shaft to the club head

Hosel Rocket – The shot that flies away at an unintended angle after a shank

Hybrid – An increasingly popular club that looks like a wood but strikes like an iron, offering greater forgiveness, useful for hacking out of the rough

Hussain, Saddam – To go from bunker to bunker

Hudson, Rock – Thought it was straight, but it wasn't

Hustler – *Derog.* The golfer who downplays his skill levels to win money. 'Titanic' Thompson - gambler, murderer, conman - was the undisputed master of this dark practice. Playing scratch off both hands, Titanic played at wealthy country clubs, winning right-handed for a small sum, then offering to play left-handed for much more. 'The best shotmaker I ever saw,' said the great Ben Hogan. See **Also Bandit, Sandbagger**

I J K

Iffy Lie – i) A disheartening position from which to take a shot ii) 'I did NOT side-foot my ball out of that deep rough!'

Impact, The Moment of – What it all comes down to, the micro-second when club strikes ball. After all that coaching and club-waggling, the silence on the tee box, that visualisation of the ball rifling away into a blue sky, joy or despair awaiting. Is it a good shot or a duff? Is it going straight down the fairway, rocketing towards the shrubbery, or dribbling off the tee? Are you going to be feeling like Tiger Woods or Mr Bean?

Impact Bag – Foam-filled training sack, the golfer's punch bag, for honing the swing and set-up, building muscle memory, and growing your game. To be slapped repeatedly until numb with boredom or suffering delusions of golfing greatness. Most bags see a great deal of use in the garage for a few days after

Christmas, later to be found lying around gardens or in the mouths of large dogs

Iron Byron – A robotic machine once used by manufacturers to test balls and clubs, programmed to execute the most efficient and consistent swing. As its operating template, the inventors copied the swing of US golfer Byron 'Lord Byron' Nelson, considered to have had the most consistently straight drive in history

Jail, In – When the ball is trapped in an impossible position, and the player can't swing at it, e.g. in the roots of a tree, wedged beneath a rock, under the beer van

James Joyce Putt – A challenging read. See also **Salman Rushdie**

Jar!, In the – When the putt is sunk into the cup

Jerk – i) When a putt immediately sets off in the wrong direction ii) The crowing guy who has just beaten you hands-down and is giving you some handy tips on your technique or attitude over the beer you've just bought him

Jigger - *Arch.* Old-school, versatile club, a pitching wedge or an early form of hybrid, used for a variety of shots. Lovely word, shame obsolete. Origin uncertain but likely refers to the little measuring cup used by bartenders to add various spirits to a glass

Jones, Vinnie – *Brit.* When the ball takes an unexpectedly nasty kick. Named for the English soccer hardman who liked to give his opponents a little tap on the ankles off the ball when the referee was looking the other way, just to let them know he was there

Juicy Lie – i) When the ball sits lovely and flush ii) 'Yes, it was a fun day. I went round in four over, won the pot and shot a hole-in-one on the difficult 17th.'

Jungle – Deep rough. See also **Cabbage, Goat's Breakfast, Spinach**

Kate Moss – A shot that's a bit thin. See also **Fat Shot**

Keep the Lag – Holding the wrist hinge of the left hand at the moment of impact to 'hit down' and 'trap' the ball rather than just slapping it. i.e. not releasing too quickly

Kitty Litter – Bunker. See also **Cat Box**

Knee-knocker – Tense, nerve-jiggering putt

Knife – A 1-iron, or Driving Iron. A.k.a. Butter knife

Knockdown Shot – Played with less than a full swing to control distance, trajectory and spin when the wind is up, there's an obstacle to negotiate, or the ground conditions encourage it. See also **Punch Shot**

Knock-off Clubs – Counterfeit clubs passing off as one of the superior brands

Kournikova, Anna – Looks tremendous but unlikely to end with a successful result. Named for the glamorous Russian tennis player who never won a Singles title

L

Lag Putt – A long one to get in the neighbourhood of the cup and leave a short and easy second. See also **Depth Charge**

Lake Ball – Ball that has been recovered from a water hazard, refurbished and sold on. It's big business!

Lateral Slide – A term of little interest to the casual golfer, though he probably violates its principles every shot. This relates to the rotation and shifting of the hip position in the downward swing

Laurel & Hardy – Fat shot followed by a thin one or vice versa

Lawn Dart – When a high-arcing ball impales the turf and goes no further

Lay the Sod – Hit the earth before the ball

Lay Up – The approach-shot equivalent of a **Lag Putt**, playing the percentages, leaving the shot short of the green to avoid an obstacle or hazard or reduce the risk. Some golfers adopt laying-up as a game strategy, seeing discretion as the better part of valour

Leaderboard – The happy place where all professional golfers like to see their name

Leather, In the – A putt close enough to the hole to merit a 'gimme' by the opponent. It originates from the old practice of measuring the distance to a hole with the leather grip of the club

Le Pen – Too far right. After far-right French politician Marine Le Pen and for an older generation of golfers, her father, Jean-Marie

Let the Big Dog Eat – Using the Driver

Lie – i) Where the ball settles ii) Any tale of course heroics, usually told at the end of a decent clubhouse lunch

Like a Butterfly – When the ball lands gently on the green

Links – Common in the UK, the terrain and location of these historic coastline courses make them rougher and tougher than inland ones. Harsher weather and strong winds demand a unique style of game and often make for a bracing day out. Favoured by hardier golfers up for a challenge

Lip – i) Rim of the bunker or hole ii) What your opponent gives you if you offer him some advice on his swing or stance

Local Rule – An additional rule peculiar to a course owing to exceptional conditions. e.g. At Pebble Beach, California, a player can replace his ball without penalty if a seagull takes off with the original. At the Royal Melbourne, a player is permitted to move his ball if it lands on an anthill

Locking the Knee – When the trailing knee remains rigid in the follow-through. Don't do this, is the advice

Loft - The angle between the clubface and the shaft, more pronounced in wedges for a steeper parabola

Long Game – As opposed to the 'short game' around the greens, the long game refers to the play in the first part of a hole in which a player seeks to achieve as much distance as possible from the tee and along the fairway

Loop – Caddie shack talk for a round

Looper – Caddie. He goes round and round

Lost Ball – One more addition to the countless millions littering the surface of the earth, choking shrubbery and swathes of long grass

Low Shot – i) Played in windy conditions or down a narrow or tree-flanked fairway ii) Snide comment out of the side of the mouth after a partner's poor shot, or in reference to his new golfing slacks

Lumberjack – *Derog.* The player in and out of the trees during a round

M

Mallet – Putter with a large head

Mashed Potatoes! – Irksome term yelled by spectators at Pro tournaments, meaning roughly, 'Way to Go!' or 'Get in the hole!' It has spawned more, equally daft iterations, notably 'Cheeseburger!' The craze is said to have started at a tournament in 2011 when Tiger Woods was teeing off and a fan shouted it so that his mother, watching on TV, knew he was there

Mashie – Before the numbering of clubs was introduced, clubs went by names. A Mashie would be a five or six iron today; the mid-Mashie a three; the Mashie Niblick a seven. Like so much of golf culture, the roots of this term lie obscured in the deep mists of Scottish history

Matchplay – Hole-by-hole competition rather than the total number of strokes in a round. As played in the Ryder Cup

Member's Bounce – The favourable fall and roll of the ball. Like the mid-morning 'Chairman's train' to town, only the most privileged get to benefit from this perk of status. See also **Goldie**

Michael Jackson – Of a shot gradually fading

Mickey Mouse Course – *Derog*. Annoying little course with short holes fit only for kids and cartoon characters. See also **Toytown**

Misread – When a golfer has spent two minutes on his haunches, then walks back and forth over the green, chin in hand, like he's working out a solution to the Middle East question, and finally hits his putt ten feet wide of the hole

Moment of Inertia – i) Technical reference to the design of a club measuring its resistance to twisting. A phrase of absolutely no interest or help to the casual golfer ii) Moment in the rough on the 14th under a grey sky when you pause and wonder what on earth you are doing with your life

Mouth Wedge – A gobby golfer who talks too much and bugs hell out of his playing partners

Mudlark – Or Mudder. A player who excels on a wet course

Mulligan – Commonly used term of uncertain origin, the Mulligan is a second shot granted to a player on the first tee without penalty after making a hash of his first. The word has been traced back to many useless players called Mulligan in the early twentieth century, but his true identity remains a mystery

Muni - Municipal course owned and maintained by the local authority for the use of ordinary people, i.e. those unable to afford exorbitant members' fees or who have been quietly blocked from joining the club because their face doesn't quite fit

Muscleback – A specialised, less forgiving type of iron used by more skilled players with a small sweet spot or 'muscle' behind the clubface. See Also **Blade**

N

Nassau – A three-part golf bet with money on the front nine holes, the back nine and the full eighteen. The term probably originates from the historic Nassau County Club on Long Island

Net Score – Score for the round minus the handicap from the gross score

Never In – When a golfer falls short with his putt and knows it even before he takes the shot

Niblick – *Arch.* Name for high-lofted old club, equivalent to a modern 9-iron

Nice putt, Alice! – A golfing misnomer based on phonetic confusion. Strictly, it is, *Alliss!* Not *Alice!* - a reference to Peter Alliss, the BBC's 'Voice of Golf', used mockingly when someone misses an easy putt, as Alliss did in the 1963 Ryder Cup and a wag in the crowd shouted, 'Nice putt, Alliss!'

Nineteenth, The – The clubhouse bar where pints are sunk nervelessly, and everyone plays off scratch. The casual golfer's favourite and most successful hole

Nuked – When a drive is struck with enormous power

O

OJ Simpson – Very bad indeed but got away with it

On the Charge – What a player is said to be when he is nailing his birdies and surging up the leaderboard. Such a player is distinguishable by his purposeful march down the fairway, chest out, shoulders back, slapping his leather glove into his palm like an SS officer

On the Nut - Bang in the sweet spot

Oscar Brown – *U.S.* OB, Out of Bounds, obscure reference to 20th-century US actor, writer and activist. See Alec Guinness for a term of equally abstruse origin

Out of the Screws – Another expression golf has donated to the wider world. Meaning 'in the sweet spot' or hit flush, the term goes back to the days when clubheads were made from wood with a thin metal covering screwed into the face

Outside Takeaway – Swing issue caused by one or more mechanical malfunctions flowing from a player's inexperience or chronic ineptitude

Over the Top – Another form of malfunction with the club outside the 'ideal swing'. Ask a coach

Overclub – Always an amusing spectacle for the bitter rival, this occurs when a player chooses a club too big for the shot, the ball shooting past the intended target. This will often happen when a player has been under-clubbing or striking poorly all day and, overcompensating, his judgement swings too far the other way

Overswing – Pulling the club too far back over the shoulders, causing a loss of balance and control, and ending wretchedly with the shot of a drunkard

P Q

Patrons – Pompous, awkward term used by the Augusta National to describe the mob of fans descending on their beautiful Georgia course to watch the Masters tournament. (To 'behold' the Masters, surely?) Hard to square 'patron' with the drunk guy whooping his mouth off at the tee-off

Paula Radcliffe – *Brit.* A ball that runs a long way, after British marathon champion

Peach Fuzz – The area around the green where the grass is slightly longer. See also **Apron, Fringe, Frog Hair**

Pedestal Green – A picturesque putting green substantially raised above its surroundings, characterised by steep slopes leading to it and presenting a formidable challenge to the golfer on the approach

Pesci, Joe – A mean little five-footer. See also **Diego; Devito, Danny**

Pin High – A confusing term that has nothing to do with height, and no golfer, coach, or commentator has ever been able to explain it with great accuracy or authority. In short, it means to get your ball very close to the hole, i.e. about a flagstick's length away

Pitch and Run – Lightly lofted wedge shot played with the aim of a gentle landing and a light roll toward the pin

Playing Through – When the idlers and incompetents playing the hole in front extend the courtesy of allowing the frustrated group behind to overtake them. A common cause of diplomatic tension on courses and clubhouses the world over

Plugged Lie – When a ball, usually from on high, buries half or more of itself in sand or undergrowth

Postage Stamp – A small, tight green

Princess Grace – Should have taken a driver

Provisional – A backup ball played when the original is feared to be out of bounds. The

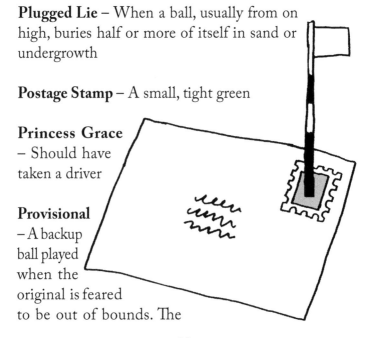

rules allow for a second one in case the original cannot be found. The rule aims to keep the game moving. See **Gerry Adams, Happy Ball**

Punch Shot – Usually played to avoid overhanging branches, struck with minimal backswing for a low flight path. Also useful in strong winds. See also **Knockdown**

Push the Ball – When a ball continues to fly in the direction it was struck but forgets to curve back

Q School – Qualifying tournament

Quadruple – A bogey of four shots over par. See **Snowman**

Quail-High – A ball flying just above the ground in a fashion similar to the flight of the ground-dwelling game bird of the pheasant family

Quintuple – A bogey of five shots over par. See **Abominable Snowman**

Quitting the Swing - When a player slows the down-swing rather than accelerates into the follow-through. See **Decel**

R

Rabbit – *Derog.* One of roughly 400 second-tier professionals who must play in qualifying tournaments to win a spot in the main event

Rainmaker – High shot with a very steep parabola, played deliberately to clear an obstacle or land the ball with minimal roll – or a dreadful one unintended by the Duffer

Range Ball – Lower quality ball, often with an identifying stripe, for use on the driving range. The less confident golfer will use one on a challenging hole thick with rough

Range Finder – A handheld viewing gadget that calculates the distance to the pin or another feature on the course with remarkable accuracy. Useful only for the casual player so that he can guess by roughly how much he will miss the target. Its removal from a player's bag has been known to provoke mutterings of 'All the kit but still shit.'

Read the Greens – Micro-navigation of the putting surface ahead of a long shot, assessing the contours, grain and gradient to determine which way the ball will likely break and run. See **Misread**

Ready Golf – Term to describe the policy of playing the ball whenever it is safe to do so rather than waiting for the hindmost, the aim being to round the course as quickly as possible and head off the frustrations of the group behind

Recovery Shot – A good effort to remove the ball from an awkward situation into a playable one. Examples include a **Bump & Run** or a **Punch Shot** from under a shady bower

Red October – A ball in the water you'll never find

Redknapp, Harry – *Brit. Cru.* Twitchy in the set-up. Named for the former English football manager. A cruel term because Redknapp developed his minor tic after a terrible road accident during the 1990 World Cup in which his friend died

Release – i) Unhinging the wrists into the fol-low-through of the swing ii) The feeling experienced after sinking a putt on the sixth attempt

Reload – When you take another ball after the first effort has plunged into a lake or disappeared amongst the livestock of a neighbouring field

Rescue Club – A hybrid or utility club to help the player in a desperate situation, usually deep rough. See also **Hybrid**

Reverse Pivot – i) Error in the swing when golfer shifts his weight incorrectly ii) Balletic pirouette performed by a disappointed player who has just witnessed a crucial putt lip out

Rickshaw – Pull-cart with big tyres

Rough – Hostile territory flanking a fairway populated by angry, primitive players scything and kicking at the grass, bellowing at the heavens and vowing never to play another round of golf in their lives. See also **Broccoli Beater, Cabbage, Goat's Breakfast, Spinach**

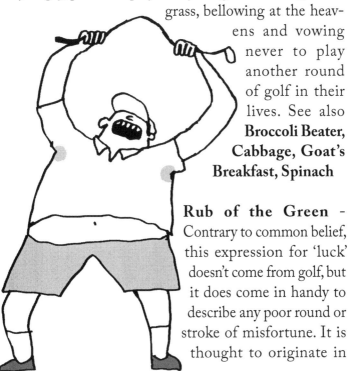

Rub of the Green - Contrary to common belief, this expression for 'luck' doesn't come from golf, but it does come in handy to describe any poor round or stroke of misfortune. It is thought to originate in

lawn bowls in 15th-century England. As Hamlet says, 'There's the rub'.

Rules of Golf – Golf's legal constitution written and administered jointly by the UK's R&A and the US Golf Association

Rushdie, Salman – An impossible read. See also **James Joyce**

Ryanair Shot – *Brit.* Not bad in the air, but landing miles from the intended destination

S

Sandbagger – Devious bounder who lies about his ability or plays poorly in recreational games to raise his handicap and gain an advantage in more serious competitions and win bets. See Also **Hustler, Bandit**

Sand Save – Getting out of the bunker and holing with one putt

Sandy, Gone – In the bunker

Scargill, Arthur – *Brit.* Great strike but will not lead to a positive outcome. Named for the Miners' Union leader and scourge of the government in the 1980s

Sclaff – To strike the ball very ineptly, specifically to extract some turf when the club hits the ground behind the ball

Scooping the Ball – Amateurish effort to get some loft on a ball, usually resulting in a useless limp chip, the ball dolloped a few yards forward like a spoonful of dessert. The sort of hapless shot shown in a comedy sketch

Scramble – i) Game format in which the best shot is selected, and all the players then take theirs from that position, making for a quicker round and sparing the blushes of the weakest player ii) When a player fails to make the 'green in regulation' (i.e. two strokes below par) but recovers with excellent short-game work to make par or better

Scratch Golfer – First-class player with a handicap of zero. The term comes from the early days of Sport when starting lines were marked with a scratch in the dirt, i.e. 'starting from scratch.'

Set-up – Twitching, waggling, sighing, frowning, head-shaking, lip-puckering, foot-shuffling, sticking the bum out: the ritual choreography a player performs getting ready to address the ball

Shaft – i) The long bit of the golf club connecting hands to clubhead ii) What the **Sandbagger** or **Bandit** does to his playing partners

Shag Bag – Handbag for collecting and storing practice balls. Nothing to do with the British slang word for a bit of slap-and-tickle, the word comes from its original meaning to 'chase after and gather.' Baseball players also shag

Shagging – Stop it! In the golf world, this means collecting balls from the practice area. A 'shagger' is the job description of the man picking up the balls

Shank – Poor shot when the Hosel, not the clubface, makes the contact; the ball splutters a short distance and veers away at an unwelcome angle. A repeat offender is said to be suffering from 'the shanks'

Shark – A player who makes par despite his ball taking a dive in the water

Shoot Your Temperature – A round of 97 or 98

Short Game – Part of the game played on the approach to, and on, the green. Players are said to have a 'good short game' often as a diplomatic way of saying that their long game is wanting

Shot Shaping – Deliberately controlling the curvature of the ball's trajectory with draw and fade, hook and slice, in order to negotiate obstacles or the lie of the land

Shotgun Start – i) Format in which players tee off simultaneously from different holes. Back in the day, a shotgun was used to signal the start. Today, it is a horn or klaxon ii) Starting a round from a hole further along the course

Short Swing – i) Abridged version of the full monty, played with minimal backswing and follow-through for more control over a short distance ii) Classic swing of the

Duffer, an ugly stab at the ball as if putting a wounded animal out of its misery

Side Saddle – Putting stance when feet point to the hole rather than, as usual, straight out from the body, addressing the ball

Side Salad – Light rough

Silly Season – Period outside the Pro tour season when players get to fill their boots and swag bags at entertainment money tournaments

Sister-in-law Shot – *Vulg.* This is a family entertainment. Ask a friend

Skied Shot – Ball hit ludicrously high in error

Skins – Format for money or points, hole-by-hole. The term's origin is uncertain, but it is probably related to 'skinning' a person for money. The claim it derives from hunters and trappers playing for pelts and hides is self-evidently preposterous. When did you last see a fur trapper come in from the wild for a round of golf?

Skull – When you hit the crown of the ball and watch the delinquent effort skip and hop a short distance over the grass. See also **Topped**

Slap the Ball – Failing to hit through the ball with a full swing, so giving it a cuff rather than the full haymaker

Slice – A common sight in a round of casual golf, the ball veering away extravagantly to the right (for a right-handed player) owing to mechanical failings of the player's set-up and swing. You could write a book …

Slope Rating – System to measure the difficulty of a golf course for non-scratch golfers, helping to calculate a player's handicap index and skill levels wherever they play. The scale runs from 55 to 155, with 113 considered a course of average difficulty

Smash Factor – Measurement of the ratio between club head speed and ball speed. i.e. the transfer of energy to the ball. The monitoring device is a gadget of questionable utility for the casual golfer more worried about just landing the damned thing on the fairway

Smoked – Hit jolly hard and far

Snake – i) Meandering putt over a large green ii) A player who can't sink his putt, the ball slithering back and forth all over the green

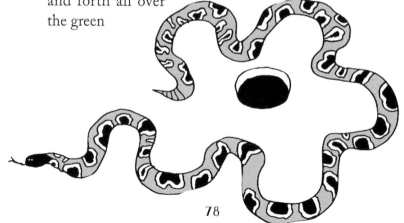

Snake Farm – U.S. Area of rough on hot-climate courses inhabited by serpents

Snipe – A shooting ball that skims the fairway and drops fast to the ground, often in the rough, in the manner of the low-flying game bird of the same name fleeing for cover from gunmen and other predators

Snowman – Score of eight on a hole. You can work that out

Sole – i) Underside of the iron ii) Catch-of the-day in the better clubhouses

Son-in-law – Of a shot you weren't really hoping for, but it will just about do. i.e. It's in the light rough or a bit short of the green, or not completely plugged in the bunker or rough. In a similar way, the golfer is happy that his son-in-law is not an ex-con or a junkie

Spinach – The Rough. See also **Cabbage, Goat's Breakfast, Jungle**

Spoon – *Arch.* The equivalent of a 5-wood, so called owing to its concave face

Sprachle – *Sco.* Lovely ancient Scots term for clambering clumsily and, on a golf course, to be playing badly

Stableford – Scoring system by which the number of strokes on a hole, relative to par and handicap, is converted into points, the aim being to achieve the highest number of points rather than the lowest score, encouraging faster and riskier play. Named for its inventor, British doctor Frank Stableford, to deter players from giving up hope after a couple of bad holes

Stem the Bleeding – Good shot that ends a terrible period of play

Sticks – Cool guy's term for his clubs

Stimpmeter – Device to measure the speed of balls over putting greens. Named for its inventor, Edward Stimpson, former golf captain at Harvard

Stinger – A favourite of Tiger Woods, a shot for greater control in strong winds, the ball hit fast and low

Stroke Play – Standard scoring system by which the player around the course in the least amount of strokes, wins. No maths skills or calculators needed

Sucker Pin – A trap for the cocky player, this is where the hole has been placed extremely close to a bunker, water hazard or precipitous slope

Sunblocker – Golfer spending an excessive amount of time **'On the Beach'** in the bunker

Sunday Bag – Lightweight golf bag, just a few essential clubs and accessories, easy on the back and shoulders. See also **Carry Bag**

Sunday Stick – *Arch.* Or Sabbath Stick. A club disguised as a walking cane from the time when golf on a Sunday was banned or frowned upon. Sold strongly in the more austere Presbyterian regions of Scotland

Super – *Abbrev.* i) Superintendent or greenkeeper ii) When you're playing like Seve Ballesteros on crack, and your opponent like a **Duffer**

Swale – Poetic word for a depression or hollow on the fairway

Sweet Spot – Smack in the middle of the club, good contact, straight **Out of the Screws**

Swing Oil – Booze consumed during a round

Swing Plane – Imaginary representation of the path of your swing. Unhelpfully, a coach will often tell you, 'Just picture a tilted aircraft.' Standard reply: 'No, still getting nothing.'

Swing Thought – A mental prompt or mantra to help a player execute a particular shot.: 'Keep the Lag… Hold the Tray… Swing the hose… Throw your belt buckle at it! … You can't make an omelette without breaking some eggs… Hit down on it, you fool …' Whatever works

T

Takeaway – The start of the backswing after addressing the ball. Get it wrong here, and calamity will be sure to follow

Target Golf – A specific game in its own right, hitting nets and marked areas, this is also a new-ish expression to meet the modern trend in golf design for more hazards, narrower fairways and smaller greens, inviting a more cautious and precise playing strategy. The player aims for particular areas in their advance to the green in the manner of children playing Grandma's Footsteps

Tee Box – The launchpad for every hole, the designated rectangle where the fun and frustration begins

Tee Markers – Painted stones, logs, branded signs, cheap plastic junk, anything that demarcates the area on the tee in which the first shot is taken

Tending the Flag – Holding the flagstick in the hole to remove it after the player has putted. A small, dull book might be written about the recent hullaballoo over changes to the rules governing flag-tending

Tester – i) The person employed to try out golf clubs and equipment before they go to market ii) Tough shot or putt

Texas Wedge – Using the putter from outside the green. Why 'Texas'? Possibly because the Lone Star State is the go-to descriptor in America for any form of behaviour that is considered a little wild or gung-ho, similar to the British use of the word 'Irish' for anything unorthodox. Possibly because courses in Texas used to be drier and harder than most, the grasser thinner, inviting the pre-mature use of the putter

Thin shot – Striking high on the ball towards the crown, resulting in the ball dribbling or scooting just a few yards forward, to the shame and fury of the executor

Three Jack – Three-putt effort

Three-quarter Shot – When a player, usually in the approach shot, deploys a roughly 75 per cent swing and follow-through to gain greater control and avoid flying over the green

Through the Green – Called the 'General Area' in Golf's rules since 2019, this refers to all areas of a hole or course other than the teeing area, the hazards and the green—the fairway, rough and trees, in other words.

Tiger Line – A nod to the great man, Woods. Hitting from the tee straight off for the green on a Par 4, heedless of all obstacles in the ball's path. Ballsy approach to a hole

Tiger Slam – Winning all four Majors in a career, a feat achieved by only five players: Tiger Woods, Jack Nicklaus, Gary Payer, Ben Hogan, and someone called Gene Sarazen, unknown to anyone under the age of 70

Tight Lie – Ball on a very close-mown fairway

Tips – Patronising advice from the smug

Toe – The top end of the clubface. The sweet spot for many a casual golfer

Tony Hart – *Brit.* When the ball has drawn. After English artist and children's TV entertainer best known for his animated character Morph

Top Edge – The visible, high end of the club head to which the golfer addresses his final prayers before the shot

Topped – Hitting the crown of the ball. See also **Skull**

Toytown – *Brit.* A derisory term for low-quality courses fit only for cartoon characters like Larry the Lamb, Derek the Daschund and Mr Growser the Grocer from the popular UK children's radio show. See Also **Mickey Mouse**

Tree Shot – A shot inconvenienced by the thoughtless planting of tall, woody perennial plants

Tree-hugger – The player forever hitting into the tree line. See also **Backwoodsman**

Tree Trouble – A ball heading for the woods or lost in their gloom

Trap the Ball – A popular **Swing Thought**, meaning to hit down on the ball. That's a good thing

Turkey – Three consecutive birdies. Term thought to be taken from ten-pin bowling, so called because, in the early 20th Century, a turkey was awarded in tournaments to anyone who achieved three consecutive strikes

The Turn – The hinge point of an 18-hole course, leaving the **Front Nine** for the **Back Nine**. In a reversal of the poker sequence, in golf, the Turn is often followed by the Flop

U

Underclub – Choosing a club with insufficient loft or incapable of making the distance. The margins between over-clubbing and under-clubbing are fine. It's why caddies have jobs

Unplayable – When a ball has come to rest, and its removal with a decent swing of a golf club is a physical impossibility, e.g. in a thicket of brambles, down a rabbit hole, at the foot of a wall, inside the beer van

Up and Down – When a player, off the green, completes the hole in two strokes

Upslope – Describing the incline of the ground over which the ball must travel when the player has the awkwardness of addressing it with his feet below. N.B. Don't ever say 'Uphill'! Downslope presents the difficulty in reverse

V

Valleys – The dips and hollows in an undulating fairway. See also **Swale**

Velcro – A slow, sticky green, after the furry fastening tape

Victory Lap – When a putt completes a circuit of the hole's lip before dropping in, occasioning relief and celebrations

WXYZ

Waggle – The dance of the club head in the ritual of **Addressing the Ball** before the shot

Wall Street – The 'bailout area' on a hole, or pain-free option, offering the golfer the opportunity of taking a risk-free alternative to investing in a more hazardous line

Waste Bunker – i) Unofficial bunker, usually a sandy, rocky area ii) A sand bunker visited by cats and dogs

Water Ball – The crappy old ball the unconfident golfer uses so as not to lose his good one in the water hazard

Watery Grave – Any form of water hazard where your poorly struck ball goes to see out eternity

Wedgie – i) Slang for any form of wedge club ii) Yanking someone's underpants up through their buttock cheeks, a sight rarely seen on the better golf courses

Wenger, Arsene – When everyone saw where the ball went except the player himself. Refers to French former manager of Arsenal football club, who could never recall seeing infringements or fouls committed by his players

Whiffing – A swing and a miss at the ball provoking mortification and self-loathing

Whins – *Sco.* Area of heavy rough covered in spiny gorse bushes commonly found in Scotland

and other regions of the UK and Ireland. The dramatic sight of the expanse of bright yellow flowers is lost on the golfer whose ball is travelling towards it

Windcheater – Successful low shot that has got the better of the strong gusts to travel where it was intended

Wire-to-Wire – When a player leads a tournament from the first tee to trophy

Wise, Dennis – *Brit.* A nasty little five-footer. Of a putt. Named after the spiky and aggressive Chelsea and England footballer

Woodie – When a player makes par after striking a tree

Worm-burner – A mishit that shoots along the ground

X, Make an – Picking up the ball before finishing a hole, generally in a huff, and marking an X on the card

Yank – i) Shot pulled to the left ii) Member of the US Ryder Cup team

Yardage, Good – Of a drive that has eaten up some distance

Yasser Arafat – Ugly, and in the sand

Yips – Unfortunate condition of uncertain cause that affects golfers and players in highly-skilled, hand-eye sports by which they become paralysed by doubts and indecision and freeze up. It can be a serious problem and affect even the best players like Ben Hogan, Sam Snead and Bernhard Langer

Zinger – A shot struck hard and high on the ball, resulting in a very fast low trajectory

Zoomie – A surprisingly long drive

Acknowledgements

Since the publication of Badger's Cricket Compendium a few months earlier, our illustrator Mudd Bexley has been shortlisted for the 2024 World Illustration Awards: an incredible achievement, especially for someone so young, but no surprise. She's a tremendous talent and once again, I am bowled over by the wit and quality of the illustrations she has produced here, perfectly capturing the whimsical tone of a book that is meant, above all, to be a bit of harmless fun. She is a delight to work with. It would be no surprise if, by the time you read this, she goes the whole way, beats off international rivals and takes the big prize itself.

Thanks also to Rebecca Brown and Andrew Brown, the brilliant and highly efficient cover and interior designers at Principal Publishing. There is little they don't know about the design, production and publication of books. I thank them also for their patience in fielding the dozens of questions I hurl their way. Like Mudd, they too have the gift of instantly capturing the tone of a book, bringing the content to graphic life with wit and precision.

About the Author

Niall Edworthy is one of the UK's leading ghostwriters. He started his career as a cricket reporter for the Independent on Sunday before joining the international wire agency AFP and later Reuters, reporting on news and sport.

He began writing books in 1997. His first was a history of the England football team, the second a history of Lord's cricket ground, and his first collaborative project, a book with the Only Fools and Horses actor David Jason.

He has since written over forty titles, the majority of them ghosted for well-known names: actors, musicians, sportsmen & television personalities, but also several notable servicemen and 'ordinary' people with extraordinary stories to tell.

His first novel, *Otto Eckhart's Ordeal*, was shortlisted for the Wilbur Smith Best Published Novel Award 2021. He has recently finished his second novel. He lives in West Sussex, UK.

Contact: niall@nialledworthy.com

If you enjoyed *Badger's Golf Compendium*, you might also enjoy *Badger's Cricket Compendium: A Humorous Illustrated Treasury of Phrase & Foible*.

NIALLEDWORTHY.COM

Printed in Great Britain
by Amazon

52208738R00065